Hi and Lois®

BY MORT WALKER
and DIK BROWNE

HOUSE CALLS

TOR

A TOM DOHERTY ASSOCIATES BOOK

HI & LOIS: HOUSE CALLS

Copyright © 1983, 1988 by King Features Syndicate, Inc.

First printing: April 1988

A TOR Book

Published by Tom Doherty Associates, Inc.
49 West 24th Street
New York, NY 10010

ISBN: 0-812-56922-9
Can. No.: 0-812-56923-7

Printed in the United States of America

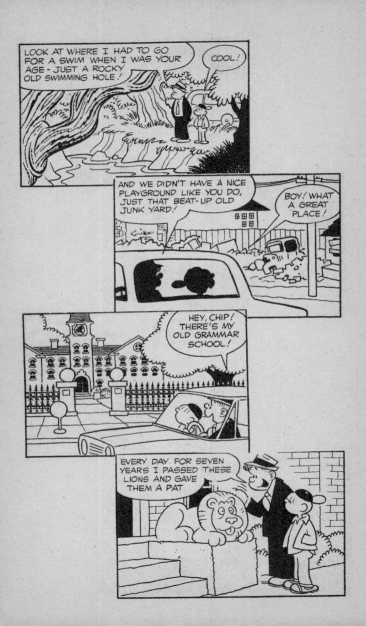

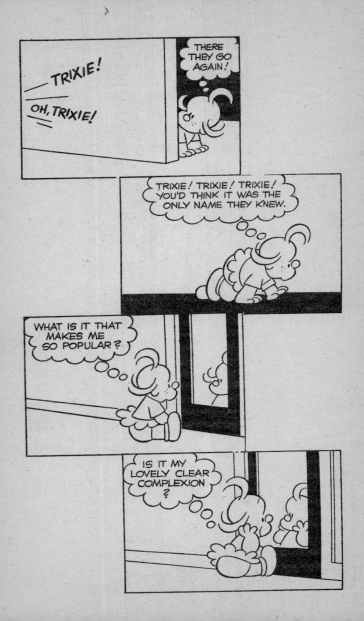

BEETLE BAILEY
THE WACKIEST G.I. IN THE ARMY